UNUSUAL FRIENDSHIPS

Symbiosis in the Animal World

UNUSUAL FRIENDSHIPS

Symbiosis in the Animal World
by
Larry Dane Brimner

FRANKLIN WATTS

New York/Chicago/London/Sydney

A FIRST BOOK

Remembering A. Brad Truax, M.D.

And dedicated to the San Diego AIDS Foundation—
it's about friendships.

Photographs copyright ©: Cover: Mickey Gibson/Animals Animals; Frontis: Dale & Marian Zimmerman/Animals Animals; 9: Will Troye/Visuals Unlimited; 10: George d. Lepp/Comstock; 12 (top): Frederick D. Atwood; 12 (bottom): Marty Snyderman/Visuals Unlimited; 15: Ian Beames/Ardea Photographs; 16 (top): John D. Cunningham/Visuals Unlimited; 16 (bottom): John Gerlach; 19: Carroll & Gwen Perkins; 20 (top): Oxford Scientific Films/Animals Animals; 20 (bottom): Alex Kerstitch/Bruce Coleman, Inc.; 23: Breck P. Kent; 24: Fred Bavendam; 29: Glenn Oliver/Visuals Unlimited; 30: Carl Rettenmeyer/Connecticut State Museum of Natural History; 33 (top): Anthony Bannister/Animals Animals; 33 (bottom): Peter Steyn/Areda Photographics; 36: Fred Bavendam; 39: Russ Kinne/Comstock; 40: Fred Bavendam; 43: Tom J. Ulrich/Visuals Unlimited; 44: William Grenfell/Visuals Unlimited; 47: Joe McDonald/Visuals Unlimited; 49: Carl Purcell; 50 (top): Anna Purcell; 50 (bottom): Tom McHugh/Photo Researchers; 53: Don W. Fawcett/Visuals Unlimited; 54: Stephen Ferry/Gamma-Liaison; 56: Courtesy The Seeing Eye Foundation.

Library of Congress Cataloging-in-Publication Data
Brimner, Larry Dane.
Unusual friendships : symbiosis in the animal world / by Larry Dane Brimner
p. cm—(A First book)
Includes bibliographical references and index.
ISBN 0-531-20106-6 (HC : Library binding)
ISBN 0-531-15675-3 (paperback)
1. Symbiosis—Juvenile literature. I. Title. II. Series.
QH548.B72 1993
591.52482—dc20
92-24953 CIP AC

Contents

Acknowledgments

The author is indebted to the following for
freely offering time, information,
and encouragement:

The Aquarium, Scripp's Institution
of Oceanography

John Boaz, Scripp's Institution
of Oceanography

Dr. Gerald Collier, San Diego State University

Malcolm A. Love Library,
San Diego State University

San Diego Public Library — especially the
Science Room staff, Children's Room Staff,
and the North Park branch staff.

San Diego Zoo

What Is Symbiosis?

Except when they are hunting, animals in the wild usually remain with their own kind. But have you ever heard the saying "Opposites attract"? Sometimes it's true. Sometimes certain animals associate with completely different animals and benefit from it. This is called *symbiosis*.

The term "symbiosis" was first coined by a scientist, Anton deBary, in 1876 to describe close relationships between different species. It's made from two Greek words: *sym*, which means "together," and *bios*, which means "life."

Symbiotic relationships develop for different reasons. One species may have difficulty finding food or shelter. Or it may be vulnerable to attacks by predators. Another species may provide the food or shelter, or may sound an alarm when danger is present. Thus the two different kinds of animals begin to live side by side.

While some animals know about symbiosis by instinct, others have learned it. For example, cattle egrets have learned that grazing cattle often scare up insects that hide in tall grasses. Egrets like to eat insects so they flock to where herds of cattle can be found. The cattle don't seem to mind the egrets, and the egrets find food more easily than they would if they had to search through the grass alone.

Some relationships between animals are so specialized that the individuals have developed physical adaptations that make it easier for them to be partners. Wrasse fish, for instance, have sharply pointed, angled teeth that help them to clean harmful bacteria, fungus, and parasites from "client" fish. Wrasse also have brilliant markings. Many scientists believe these markings are a type of advertising—an adaptation that helps other fish recognize them as "cleaners."

There are three kinds of symbiosis. The first, *commensalism*, occurs when one partner, the "guest," is helped and the other partner, the

The relationship between the African
buffalo and the egret is an example of
a learned symbiosis.

The osprey's nest provides a home not
only for its own young but also for
smaller birds of other species.

"host" is not helped or harmed. *Mutualism*, the second kind, is a relationship that is beneficial to both partners. And when the guest receives all the benefits and the host is harmed or destroyed, the symbiosis is called *parasitism.*

The three types of symbiosis exist all around us. You may have even seen examples and not known it. If you live along the coastal United States or Canada, you may have seen a large stick nest of an osprey that has become an "apartment house" for smaller birds. The osprey is a type of hawk that feeds mostly on fish, so it doesn't bother its guests. The smaller birds find shelter in the nooks and crannies of the osprey's nest, protection from enemies that are afraid of the large hawk, and—an added bonus—scraps of leftover food that the osprey throws away. In this commensal relationship, the osprey doesn't benefit, but it also doesn't seem to be harmed.

People and pets are another example of symbiosis. People provide a dog with shelter and food, but the dog may protect the house from unwanted intruders. Each gains something from the relationship. That's mutualism—two unlike organism receiving mutual benefits.

〈Above〉 Symbiosis exists both in the plant and the animal worlds. Mistletoe is a parasite on trees. 〈Bottom〉 The wrasse helps keep the trout free of fungus and other parasites.

Symbiosis occurs not only in the animal world, but you can also find it among plants and even bacteria, algae, and fungi. Have you ever seen mistletoe growing in a tree? Mistletoe is a parasitic plant. It lives by absorbing nutrients from the host tree. Eventually, the mistletoe may absorb all of the tree's nutrients and the tree may die.

By studying symbiosis, scientists have learned how all living things are connected. When "cleaner" fish were removed from a part of the ocean, most of the larger "client" fish disappeared within days. The few that remained became weak and ill. It seems odd that the large fish are so dependent on their small cleaners, but nature is full of odd and unusual friendships.

Friends and Enemies

Alone, an animal may not be able to defend itself from predators. It may group with others of its own kind for protection because there's safety in numbers. If any member of the group senses danger, it warns the others. But some kinds of animals lack the size, strength, speed, or sharp senses that are necessary for protection. They may need to gather with completely different animals to survive.

The long-necked ostrich and the striped zebra have a mutual enemy, the lion. As a defense, ostriches and zebras sometimes herd and feed together, one group warning the other of a prowling lion or other predator.

The largest flightless bird in the world, the black-and-white-plumed ostrich, has evolved

Although nature has given both the
ostrich and the zebra advantages for
their own defense, by banding together
the weaknesses of one are helped by
the strengths of the other.

⟨Top⟩ The zebra and the ostrich are truly an "odd couple" whose living arrangements are a success. ⟨Bottom⟩ Many of these eggs will not hatch because of predators.

powerful legs for running and can reach speeds of up to 40 miles per hour (about 64 kph). If it is cornered by an enemy, the ostrich packs a walloping, karate-style kick, slashing out with a long, sharp toenail on one of the two toes of each foot. It usually lives in large flocks on the grasslands and deserts of Africa.

In spite of their size, ostriches are vulnerable creatures. A male and three to five females take care of forty or more eggs in a ground-built nest. But a large number of the eggs will never hatch because the sitting adults can't cover them all. Other eggs will fall prey to predators. Those hatchlings that eventually escape their shells are rounded up to join the safety of the group. There, the adults' large size and lethal kicks can provide the hatchlings with some protection. Ostriches also have keen eyesight and can spot large predators long before they are close enough to attack. Still, many of the young will fall prey to jackals, leopards, and lions during their first few months. Herding with zebras can improve their chances of survival.

At one time, a zebra was thought to be a cross between a horse and a tiger. Seafaring Greeks even gave it the name *Hippotigris*, which means "horse-tiger." But zebras aren't a combination of animals. They're members of the Equidae family, to which horses and donkeys also belong, but the three varieties of zebras form their own subgroups or species.

Male zebras, called stallions, generally live together until they're ready to start their own families. Then each mates with two or more females, or mares. About a year after mating, each mare gives birth to a single offspring, or foal. At first, the foal's legs are wobbly, but it can run an hour after it's born, and mother and infant rejoin the safety of the herd.

Joining the herd is just one way that zebras protect themselves. Their stripes, which are as unique to each zebra as fingerprints are to humans, provide camouflage that helps them blend in with the tall grass and brush of their surroundings. This protects them and is known as disruptive coloration. Also, when two or more zebras stand together, they usually face in different directions to keep a lookout of enemies. They have a sharp sense of smell and good hearing. While their vision is also sharp, all animals with eyes on the sides of their heads share a weakness in judging distance. Because of this,

Zebras face in different directions so as
to spot danger from all areas.

⟨Top⟩ The Portuguese man-of-war's tentacles
may extend as much as **100** feet.
⟨Bottom⟩ Among these poisonous tentacles
safely swim the **N**omeus gronovii.

zebras sometimes gather with the sharpsighted ostrich. The ostrich, in turn, benefits from the zebra's sharper hearing and sense of smell.

Ostriches and zebras aren't the only animals in unusual friendships. Many sea animals also cooperate with each other in helpful relationships. Two of these are the Portuguese man-of-war and the man-of-war fish.

The scientific name for the Portuguese man-of-war is *Physalia physalis*, which comes from a Greek word that means "bubble." This dramatic-looking siphonophore, or jellyfish, has long tentacles that hang down from its *mantle*, or bubblelike float. The tentacles may extend to a depth of 100 feet (about 30 m), and they have stinging cells called nematocysts that can fire poisonous barbs into the man-of-war's prey.

If it weren't for a twin triggering action, the man-of-war would fire all its nematocysts every time it bumped into something. But the man-of-war's stinging cells are triggered only if something brushes up against small, hairlike projections on the tentacles and if certain chemicals are sensed at the same time.

The man-of-war fish, or *Nomeus gronovii*, takes advantage of the Portuguese man-of-war.

While most fish avoid the dangerous predator, the little Nomeus spends its whole life among the man-of-war's tentacles or close to them.

How does Nomeus live in such a dangerous way? It has acquired an immunity to the poisonous barbs, though it still may be stung if it bumps roughly against the man-of-war's tentacles. It's also a good swimmer and usually manages to avoid all but the slightest contact with them. Thus, Nomeus lives among the deadly tentacles in relative safety from predators.

Their relationship is mutually beneficial. The Portuguese man-of-war seems to use Nomeus as bait. Other fish spot Nomeus, brightly striped with blue and silver-gray, and attack it. The chase leads right back to the deadly tentacles, which the little fish swims through easily. The other fish, however, is immobilized by the man-of-war and is eaten at leisure. An added benefit for Nomeus is that it gets to feast on the man-of-war's leftovers.

Many other sea creatures exist together and benefit each other. Sea anemones, whose tentacles wave about in the currents like the petals of a flower, can be found living with a variety of companions. One of its most interesting associations is with the clown fish.

The clown fish quickly develop an
immunity to the poisonous barbs of
the sea anemone.

Clown fish never move more than a few feet away from the sea anemone. This clown fish watches over eggs laid near the beautiful purple anemone.

Clown fish, sometimes called "decoy fish" or "damselfish," are found in the coral reefs of the Indian and Pacific oceans. They measure only 3 to 6 inches (about 8 to 15 cm) in length, and stand out because of their bright orange, white, and black coloration. They swim awkwardly and have no built-in defenses against most predators. Nevertheless, clown fish have a unique way of surviving a dangerous environment. They rarely move more than a few feet from an anemone partner.

A sea anemone, like its jellyfish relatives, is armed with stinging tentacles that surround the animal's mouth. Inside each stinging cell is a coiled, hollow thread that, when triggered, is fired like a tiny harpoon. Any small creature wandering within reach of the graceful tentacles is stung, paralyzed, carried into the anemone's mouth, and eaten.

There are about eight hundred species of anemones, but only about thirteen species are suitable partners for clown fish. These are often the largest, some with a diameter greater than 3 feet (.9 m). These giant sea anemones do not depend on clown fish for survival. They are often found without clown fish. The twenty-seven known species of clown fish, on the other hand, have never been found without anemones.

Clown fish do not have a natural immunity to the stinging cells of all anemones. Each clown fish forms a lifelong partnership with a specific anemone. To do this, the clown fish performs an elaborate dance, gently touching against and then moving away from the anemone's tentacles. Before long—usually within a few hours—the clown fish can move freely among the tentacles without getting stung.

Some biologists think that the clown fish performs its dance so that it can coat its own body with mucus from the anemone. This disguises it so that the anemone doesn't recognize it as foreign. Other biologists, however, have evidence that the clown fish also produces its own protective secretion. What is known for certain is that if a clown fish goes too near the wrong anemone, it will be stung and eaten like other prey.

Like Nomeus fish and the Portuguese man-of-war, clown fish and gaint sea anemones live together with mutual benefits. The sea anemone protects the clown fish from large predators. In return, the clown fish lures prey into the anemone's tentacles, cleans it, and even defends it against bothersome butterfly fish, which are immune to anemone stings.

CHAPTER

Feasts of Sweets

For most wild animals, the search for food never ends. Some however, have learned that their search can be made easier by another animal.

One of the most interesting "food" relationships is that between the ant and the aphid. If you have very looked closely at the leaves and stems of the plants in a garden, you may have seen tiny aphids. They range in color from apple green to rust red and are sometimes called "plant lice." Their tubelike mouths puncture the outer layers of the plant stems and tap the sugary juices within the plant. They take useful nutrients from the juices, but have to consume a great deal of the sweet solution to get enough nourishment. This is why gardners dislike aphids; they can literally suck the life out of a plant!

Ants, however, find aphids useful. Wherever large colonies of aphids exist, various species of ants are often plentiful. Aphids consume more juice from the plants than they can use. The extra, called "honeydew," oozes out of their bodies, and ants find the sugary liquid appetizing. For ants, aphids represent a convenient supply of the sweet liquid.

Their relationship is very organized, with ants tending the aphids much the way a farmer tends his cows. In fact, aphids are sometimes referred to as the ants' "cows" or "cattle."

Because aphids are small and soft-bodied, they're among the most defenseless of all insects. But ants protect their "cows." One ant species shapes tiny mud huts over the aphids that shelter them from severe weather. The vicious bites of acrobatic ants, found throughout southern Canada and in the United States east of the Rocky Mountains, drives away aphid predators such as ladybugs. Many ant species move their aphids around to the juiciest parts of plants. And the ants may even take aphid eggs into their chambers through the winter.

Aphids produce honeydew naturally, but in return for care and protection they allow the ants to "milk" them. Ants do this by gently

Ants care for aphids in much the same
manner that farmers tend their cattle.

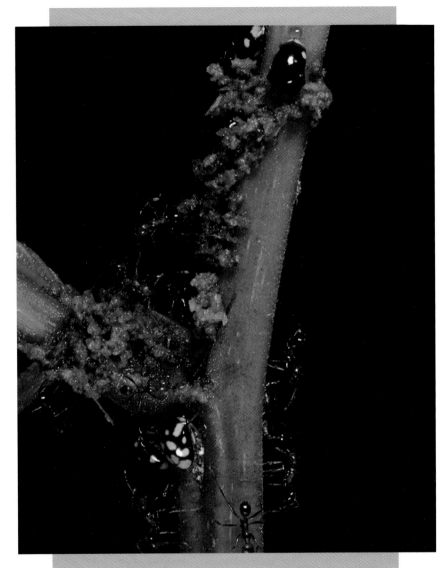

Ants care for treehoppers by
building shelters over them.

stroking the rear ends of the aphids with their antennae. This stimulates the aphids to expel their sweet liquid, which the ants lap up.

Aphids aren't the only insects that produce honeydew. Mealybugs, treehoppers, and the larvae of Australia's imperial blue butterflies can also be milked by ants. And ants are always around to take advantage of the situation.

Another sweet friendship exists between a bird and mammal found throughout much of Africa and southwestern Asia. This is the relationship between the honey guide bird and the ratel, a member of the weasel family.

The dozen species of honey guides are related to woodpeckers. They are dull brown or gray in color and have conspicuous white markings on their dark tails. They feed on insects and particularly like bees for their larvae and beeswax.

When it comes to finding bees and beeswax, honey guides are master detectives. With their sharp eyesight, they locate beehives, but use other senses as well. Honey guides can detect the smell of beeswax. They have even been reported showing up in churches where beeswax candles are burning!

Tough skins give them some immunity to bee stings, but honey guides lack the ability to tear open the beehives that they find. Two species, the black-throated and scaly-throated honey guides, find a friend to do it for them. Usually, that friend is a ratel, or "honey badger."

A ratel is a stocky animal, about 2½ feet (about .8 m) in length, and resembles a skunk with gray and white fur on its upper body and black fur below. Like a skunk, it protects itself by emitting a foul-smelling discharge from the anal glands. And it's similar to a skunk in another way, too. It will eat just about any-thing—insects, frogs, snakes, birds, and berries. But it especially likes honey, which the nocturnal ratel isn't very good at locating, at least not by itself. The ratel's good fortune is that a black-throated or scaly-throated honey guide comes looking for it as soon as the bird has located a beehive.

When it finds a ratel, the honey guide bird flits about and trills to gain the ratel's attention. Then it darts off in the direction of the beehive, stopping now and then to make sure the ratel is following. When both animals are at the bee-hive, the honey guide perches and lets the ratel go to work.

⟨Top⟩ The ratel uses its sharp claws to tear into a beehive and to eat the sweet honey inside. ⟨Bottom⟩ After the ratel has eaten its fill, the honey guide bird swoops in to feast on bees and beeswax.

With its strong forepaws, sharp claws, and powerful jaws, the ratel rips apart the hive. It isn't bothered by the angry bees; its fur protects it from stings. It eats all the honey it wants, and then waddles away. Then the honey guide swoops down and claims its bounty of bees, larvae, and beeswax.

While the honey guide's relationship with the ratel is mutual, with both animals benefiting, it has a parasitic relationship with some other birds. The honey guide doesn't raise its own young. The female lays her single white egg in the nest of another bird. When the chick hatches out of the egg, it is born with needlesharp hooks on its bill. It uses these to destroy the nestlings of the other birds. Once that's done, the hooks fall off and the young honey guide gets the full attention of its foster parents.

Help from Their Friends

Who hasn't seen apes and monkeys in a zoo groom or clean each other? One animal carefully goes through the fur of another animal, looking for and removing harmful parasites. Grooming each other is a common activity among most primates. But recently biologists have begun to realize how widespread "laundry" services are among other species of animals.

All animals need to stay clean. If they are not clean, they may become infected with disease and suffer blood loss from parasites. But some animals are physiologically not able to clean themselves. They are shaped in such a way that it's an impossible task. These animals have found some other animal to do the chore for them.

The spotted shrimp cleans the pink-
tipped sea anemone.

Cleaning symbioses are more common in the sea than anywhere else. More than forty-five species of fish are known to be cleaners. There are also six species of shrimp that provide cleaning services, as well as one type of crab, the red rock crab, which cleans ticks from marine iguanas that live in the Galapagos Islands.

At cleaning stations located in coral reefs, rocky outcrops and shipwrecks, diving biologists have seen hundreds of fishes lined up waiting for their turn to be cleaned. Typically, "cleaner" fish are smaller and tend to be brightly colored, which attracts their clients. Some even put on elaborate "dancing" displays, swimming in a vertical position with their head down to advertise their services.

Cleaning stations are well known to "client" fishes, and some clients return to the same station, sometimes even to the same cleaner, day after day. While being cleaned, clients often float at odd angles with their fins extended so that the cleaners can get to every spot. They also allow cleaners to enter their mouths and gills without trying to harm the cleaners. This symbiotic cleaning benefits both partners. The client is cleaned of bacteria, fungi, dead and diseased tissue, and harmful parasites, and the cleaner gets a meal.

Another cleaner fish, the remora, instead of setting up shop at a cleaning station, has a mobile service for fish on the go. Remoras hitchhike along with their hosts and get both a meal out of the friendship and a free ride.

Remoras are also called "sucker fish." There are several species, ranging in size from a few inches to 3 feet (.9144 m) in length. All are able to attach themselves to other objects. This is possible because they have a large oval suction disk on the top of their head.

Although remoras usually attach themselves to larger fish such as sharks, marlins, and swordfish, they have hitched rides with ships too. The disk's suction is so great that in some parts of the world fishermen use live remoras attached to their lines to catch other fish.

When remoras attach themselves to a shark, the remoras benefit from the larger fish's messy eating habits. Tiger sharks, for example, are known for their vicious attacks. They rip into their prey, tearing huge chunks of flesh from the victim. In the process, much of the

The sucking disk on the remoras head
allows it to attach itself to a shark.

This remora "hitchhikes" on the
bottom of a shark.

shark's food becomes scattered in the water. All the remoras have to do to share in the feast is let go of the shark and gobble up the scraps.

Remoras benefit in other ways, too. Hitching a ride is easier than swimming and takes them to a wide range of feeding grounds. They also get a certain amount of protection, since most other fish flee when a shark is in the neighborhood.

Sharks, however, do not gain much by their relationship with remoras. They don't benefit by sharing food or providing free rides. But they do get some benefits from the remoras. Some types of remoras remove dead skin tissue and parasitic copepoda, or small shellfish, that dig into the shark's skin.

One of the most unusual housekeeping arrangements is found on the cool, misty islands off the coast of New Zealand. The tuatara lizard, one of the earth's rarest creatures, lives here. It is the sole survivor of a group of reptiles called the rhynchocephalians, or "beak-heads," and makes its home here with the bird known as the shearwater.

The tuatara is often called a living fossil. Its ancestors were around even before most dinosaurs and have been extinct for more than 100 million years. The tuatara, however, has survived four major ice ages with only minor changes.

Named for the Maori word meaning "spine bearer," the tuatara has a row of spines down its back. Fossils indicate that it once grew to a length of about 5 feet (1.5 m). Today, the drab green insect eater measures only about 2 feet (.6 m) in length. Except for a third eye hidden in the middle of its forehead, it could be mistaken for an iguana. Unlike most other reptiles, the tuatara can remain active even when the temperature drops as low as 45° Fahrenheit (8° Celsius).

But "active" doesn't describe the tuatara. It's a sluggish, slow-moving animal. Everything it does is slow. It can even go a whole hour without breathing! It grows for half of its one hundred year life span, not mating until it's twenty years old. It reproduces only once every four to five years. A female's eggs take from twelve to sixteen months to hatch, longer than those of any other reptile. Maybe its sluggishness explains why it would rather share the burrow of the sooty shearwater than dig its own.

The spiney tuatara is a direct ancestor
of the dinosaurs and has often been
called a living fossil.

The tuatara lives in its burrow during the day, and in the evening, the shear-water (above) takes it over.

The sooty shearwater is a small, gray bird that lays its eggs, raises its young, and sleeps in an underground burrow. A sea bird, it spends it days searching for fish and returns to its burrow at night. This arrangement works well. The tuatara is a nocturnal animal, preferring to sleep during the day. When the bird returns to the nest, the tuatara is out looking for insects.

While the relationship seems one-sided, both animals benefit. The tuatara gets a burrow, but it also eats the insects in the nest that would bother the shearwater. And the tuatara may protect the eggs and nestlings of the shearwater while the adult bird fishes. (But the tuatara has also been known to eat its roommates!)

Unusual friendships crop up between animals great and small. In the wild, every giant rhinoceros is found with two or three gray-brown tickbirds for companions. As with most other symbiotic relationships, their association provides a mixture of benefits. One animal receives food and the other receives protection.

The two species of tickbirds, also known as "oxpeckers," get their entire food supply from the hides of rhinos and other large mammals in Africa. Both the yellow-billed tickbird and the red-billed tickbird are members of the starling family. They have flattened beaks for prying blood-filled parasitic ticks, flies, and larvae from the hides of their hosts. Their sharp, curved claws and stiff tails help them maintain their hold and run about in any direction. Rhinos allow their cleaning even though the tickbirds often peck at open wounds and sores.

The only time tickbirds leave their rhino host is when they're startled or when they're nesting—and even their nests are lined with the rhino's hair! Otherwise, they eat, sleep, sunbathe, court, and mate while on top of the roving rhino.

A rhino, which weighs between about 1 and 3 tons (907 and 2,722 kg), has little trouble defending itself. If it's threatened, it can charge at speeds of up to 30 miles per hour (48 kph) and can jerk its horn from the ground to a height of 7 feet (2 m) in a split second.

But defending oneself and spotting danger are two different things. While most grazing animals have excellent eyesight and can spot possible danger at some distance, rhinos are an exception. All five species of rhinoceroses are nearsighted and have trouble seeing clearly at a distance. Black rhinos' eyesight is the worst.

The tickbird cleans the much larger
rhino and serves as an early warning
system for its dim-sighted host.

They can't see more than 15 feet (4.5 m) beyond their noses.

Although rhinos have sharp hearing and a sharp sense of smell, they have come to rely on tickbirds for added protection. At the first glimpse of danger, the sharp-sighted little birds hop excitedly about the rhino, flapping their wings wildly and screeching warning calls. If that doesn't get the rhino's attention, they peck sharply on its head. Then, whether the rhino retreats or charges, the tickbirds join their unusual friend again after the danger has passed.

One of the earliest accounts of symbiosis was recorded by the Greek historian Herodotus in 459 B.C. during his travels in Egypt. He wrote about birds that entered the open jaws of crocodiles to pick out leeches and small particles of food. People have been fascinated by these birds ever since. After all, crocodiles are not known for their gentle dispositions, and they don't usually hesitate to eat birds. While most naturalists agree that Herodotus was describing the huge Nile crocodile and the Egyptian plover, they aren't certain about the accuracy of his tale.

The warm waters where Nile crocodiles spend most of their time are filled with small, flat

The cold-blooded crocodile basks
in the warm sunshine.

⟨Top⟩ The Egyptian plover bravely
dances near the crocodile's wide-opened
mouth hoping to pick out and eat parasites from the reptile's teeth. ⟨Bottom⟩
A close-up of the Egyptian plover.

worms called leeches. These pests attach themselves to the skin of another animal and feed on blood by going into the host's skin. Leeches, however, have trouble atttaching themselves to a crocodile's tough skin, so they fasten onto the softer, thinner skin in and around the mouth. This is annoying for the crocodile, which can't pick off the pest.

Like all reptiles, crocodiles are cold-blooded. That is, their body temperature is about the same as the surrounding air or water, and much of their daily life is spent cooling and warming themselves. To keep their bodies at a comfortable temperature, they climb out of the water and sunbathe on the river banks during the day. When they do, they often lie with their mouths open wide, which helps evaporation and cooling. As the crocodiles bask in the sun, Egyptian plovers dart among them and pick parsites from their backs. There are also many stories that say plovers enter the crocodiles' mouths eating and cleaning them of leeches and food debris.

The Egyptian plovers, of course, benefit from an easily available source of food. In return, they issue a shrill alarm at the first sign of danger, which sends the crocodiles scurrying into the water.

Symbiosis and People

From the very earliest times, people have had symbiotic relationships with other species. They tended and cared for sheep, protecting their flocks from predators and taking them to good pastures to graze. In return, the sheep provided people with a source of food. They also supplied wool that could be made into yarn and cloth. People today still eat lamb and wear wool clothing, and they continue to provide sheep with care and protection.

Early peoples hunted and gathered their food, but herding cows and raising chickens made it easier for them to establish permanent communities. Farmers still tend cows and chickens, and the relationship works for mutual advantage. The cows and chickens receive food

Humans have developed many beneficial relationships with animals. Here, a Navajo woman herds her sheep.

Some animals perform tasks that their
human companions cannot.

and shelter, while the farmer receives milk and eggs.

In Kenya, a part of the African continent, generations of Boran people have followed the honey guide bird to locate beehives. Like the ratel, the Boran get the honey, and the honey guide has another accomplice in its quest for beeswax.

It was a chore for American Indians to track and hunt animals for food, clothing, and shelter. But horses made them more successful hunters. And long before steam locomotives crisscrossed the United States, horses were carrying explorers and pulling wagons westward. Imagine crossing a continent on foot! Of course, some early explorers did exactly that, but horses made the journey easier. And it was faster than sailing around the tip of South America. Again, the symbiosis was mutually beneficial. Horses made life easier for people, and people treated their horses as valued possessions.

More recently, trained animals have made life easier for people. Dog guides help their blind owners get around and live independent lives. Service dogs carry supples, open doors, and flip switches for their handicapped partners. Even

The work of dog guides allows the visually
impaired greater access and freedom.

monkeys are being trained to perform useful services for people. In exchange for their services, the animals receive care and kind words. Everyone benefits from the arrangement.

Researchers are investigating other ways in which animals help people. They have found that people with pets recover more quickly from an illness than do people without pets. Evidence shows that the act of petting a dog or cat is calming and lowers a person's blood pressure. Researchers have learned that prisoners who have pets are more likely to be better behaved while in prison. Researchers, however, don't understand it all—yet. Perhaps they will someday.

Right now, they know that whether the unusual friendship is between "cleaner" fishes and their "clients" or farmers and their cows, there is a delicate balance to nature. When something upsets that balance, friendships everywhere are threatened.

Glossary

Anal gland—the opening at the end of the digestive canal; the rear end.

Antennae—the sensory "feelers" on the heads of insects.

Biologist—a scientist who studies animal life.

Boran—people native to Kenya, Africa.

Cold-blooded—animals (such as reptiles) whose body temperature is the same as the surrounding air or water.

Commensalism—two animals living together, with one benefiting and the other neither being helped nor harmed.

Copepoda—small parasitic shellfish.

Disruptive coloration—coloring that helps animals blend in with their surroundings; camouflage.

Guest—the animal receiving the benefits of a symbiotic relationship; also, the smaller of the two animals involved in a symbiotic relationship.

Honeydew—the sugary liquid that oozes out of certain insects.

Host—the larger partner in a symbiotic relationship; also, the partner that sacrifices for the other.

Larvae—immature insects in their grublike state.

Leech—a small, flat worm that sucks blood.

Maori—native people of New Zealand.

Mutualism—a symbiotic relationship in which both partners benefit.

Naturalist—a person who studies animal or plant life.

Nematocysts—stinging cells used for protection and capturing prey.

Nocturnal—active at night.

Nutrient—something that nourishes; food.

Parasite—an animal (or plant) that lives on or in another species and receives nutrients from it.

Parasitism—a symbiotic relationship in which one party is harmed or destroyed.

Predator—an animal that hunts another.

Prey—an animal that is hunted by another.

Rhynchocephalian—lizardlike reptiles that are extinct, except for the tuatara.

Siphonophore—any member of the jellyfish family.

Symbiosis—the living together of two different organisms.

Tentacle—the slender, flexible appendage of the jellyfish and sea anemone.

Tick—a small, blood-sucking parasite related to mites.

For Further Reading

Applebaum, Stan and Victoria Cox. *Going My Way?* New York: Harcourt Brace Jovanovich, 1976.

Dean, Anabel. *Strange Partners: The Story of Symbiosis.* Minneapolis: Lerner Publications, 1976.

Gotto, R. V. *Marine Animals: Partnerships and Other Associations.* London: English Universities Press, Ltd. 1969.

Hartman, Jane E. *Living Together in Nature.* New York: Holiday House, 1977.

Macquitty, Miranda, Ed. *Side by Side.* New York: G.P. Putnam's Sons, 1988.

Perry, Nicoette. *Symbiosis: Close Encounters of the Natural Kind.* England: Blandford Press, Poole, Dorset, 1983.

Prescott, Ernest. *Creatures that Help Each Other.* New York: Franklin Watts, Inc., 1976.

Silverstein, Alvin, and Virginia B. *Unusual Partners: Symbiosis in the Living World.* New York: McGraw-Hill, 1968.

Index

About the Author

Larry Dane Brimner is an award-winning author of books, stories, and articles for children. His previous Franklin Watts First Books include *Animals that Hibernate* (1991), *Karate* (1988), and *BMX Freestyle* (1987), which won the IRA "Children's Choice" award in 1988.

Mr. Brimner resides in San Diego, California.